STAFFORD CLIFF

1000 HOME IDEAS

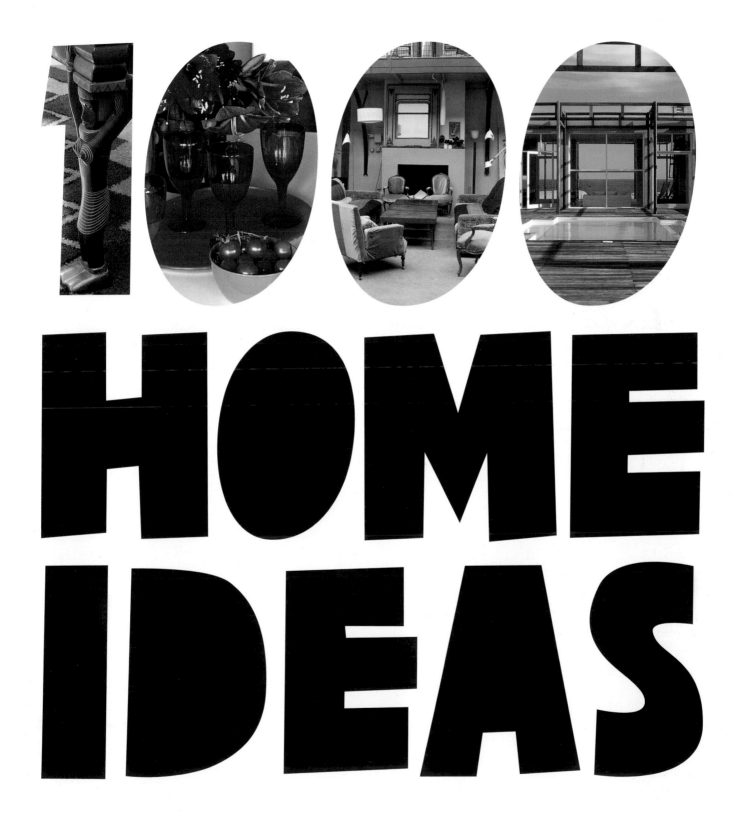

PHOTOGRAPHS BY CHRISTIAN SARRAMON

Everybody thinks about their home. When you're young, if you have your own room, it becomes your world, and you soon set about personalising it, making it your private domain. When you leave home, you start to create another one – and you wonder how you're going to manage with all the decisions you'll need to make. Some folk dread it, and others just can't wait to go shopping. But not everything is available from a shop. You'll need ideas, too. What type of floor will you have: carpets, mats, rugs or floorboards? Stone or brick, maybe? You will inherit some of the elements, and certain decisions will be made for you – by the space or the previous owners. No matter, you'll want to tailor it to your needs. Maybe you can't change the floors, the walls, the ceilings or the staircase, but you'll almost certainly need to repaint or replace some things, move them about – doors, perhaps, or even windows; an extension, a home office, a bigger bathroom. Even if the task is too big for you to undertake yourself, don't be put off. If you know the effect you want, you can easily find a local builder or craftsman to do it for you. It's all a matter of choices, and there will be dozens of them; each one you make will say something about you, or your partner – or your parents. A terrifying prospect, and one you'll need to be prepared for – not only at the start of your homemaking life, but throughout it; when you move, or when you refurnish – as your circumstances, your influences, or your income changes. The questions go on and on – but so do the answers – over 1000 of them, all collected here in the work of the brilliant French photographer Christian Sarramon – who has spent 30 years photographing some of the most extraordinary, ideas-filled homes in the world.

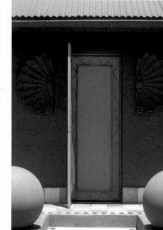

INTEREST

UNDER FOOT

I recall somebody saying to me years ago, when I moved into a new house, that 'it won't feel like a home until you've got the carpets down'. And in a sense it was true. The floor coverings softened the sound and somehow made everything feel finished, even with only one sofa and some cushions on the floor. Then, of course, there's the smell of new carpet – it's quite sensual, like the smell in a new car. But, over the past 20 years, wall-to-wall carpets have fallen out of fashion in modern interiors. Think of any of the trendy restaurants that you've been to recently, you very rarely see carpet these days. First, there was sisal: ethnic and satisfying, but difficult to clean and horrible on bare feet. And pattern was definitely out, as decorators and designers began using hard flooring: floorboards in rare woods, stone and marble. Now, a wide range of wood or wood-effect flooring is available to everyone, and people are even rescuing old floorboards from salvage yards and building sites. At the same time, stone, brick, tiles and even smooth pebbles began to be popular. These are ideal for bathrooms or areas with underfloor heating. Now, things are changing once again. Colour is back – on large 'designer' rugs with bold modern graphics, that are rather like putting a painting on the floor.

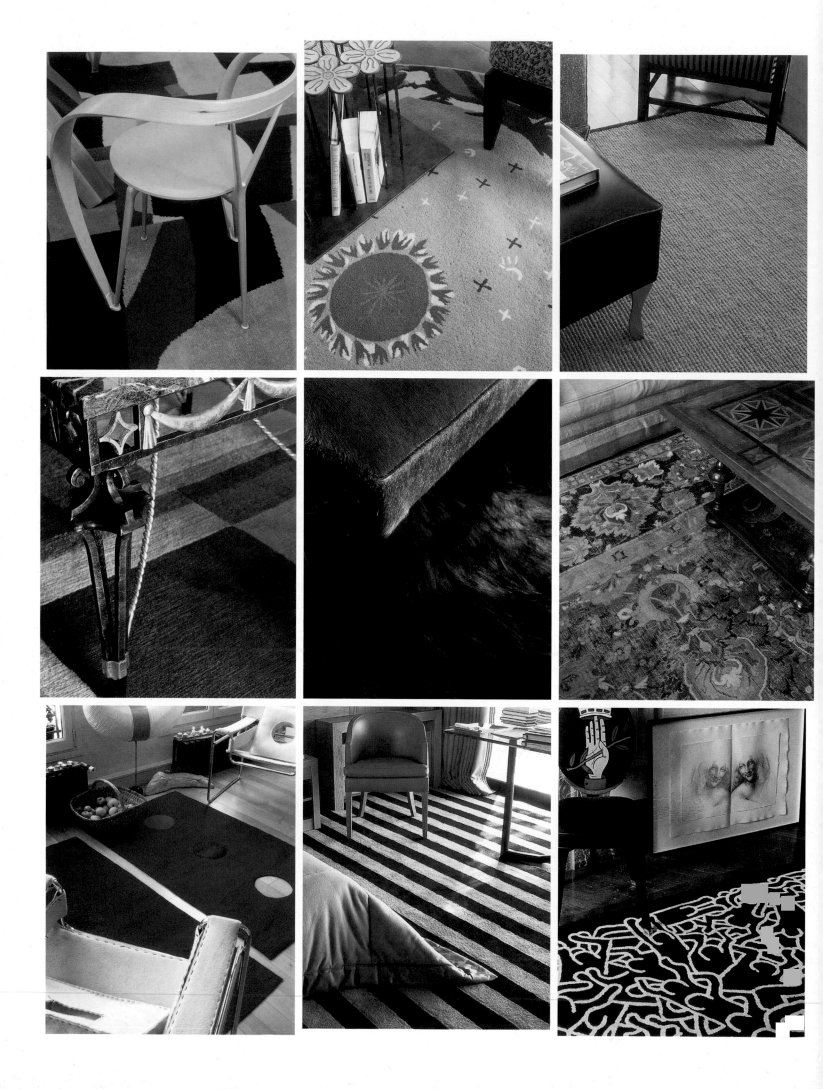

COOKING

& EATING

Our homes respond to the way we live: the stages of our life, our income and our domestic set up – single, married or a family unit. In the 1950s, the 'work triangle' concept was formulated, establishing the ideal position for the cooker, the fridge and the sink unit, so that a housewife didn't have to walk too far – if at all. Rapid changes in attitudes towards cooking, eating and entertaining, and massive advances in technology have had a bigger impact on the kitchen than anywhere else in the home. In the 1920s, the suburban kitchen was a tiny, rarely seen work station at the back of the building, but in the 1990s it was enlarged and moved to a prime position with high-tech equipment and state-of-the-art joinery. Now, with the move towards city centre living and with the abundance of tempting neighbourhood restaurants, some young people choose not to cook at all. Along the way, we had the smart modern kitchen and formal dining room, the family room with its cooking, eating, entertaining and general family life free-for-all, and the restaurant-style kitchen with its industrial-looking cookers, steamers, coffee makers and even glass-fronted fridges. None of these solutions have become inappropriate, it's up to you, your style and how you want to live.

WALLS OF

WONDER

Rooms tell many stories – as you'll know if you've ever visited the museum homes of painters, writers, collectors or famous explorers. Though no longer stuffed with the clutter of everyday life, these houses are filled with memories. If it's a house full of character, that identity will come from the person's possessions, what they collected and how it is displayed on shelves, in cabinets, on tables – or most importantly on the walls. Designers and artists love to surround themselves with pictures, paintings, prints and framed mementoes of all kinds. Explorers bring back maps, posters, bus tickets and things that remind them of their journeys. People with children will put up school drawings. But for some, having the confidence to hang things, personal things, quirky things on the walls, takes a certain bravery that they may not have. Where's the best position? What's the most suitable frame? Perhaps the solution is to concentrate first on one small space – maybe in the hall or a bedroom. Approach the wall as a page in a scrapbook rather than a gallery wall, and don't think that you have to use expensive images or one-off artworks. Displaying the most unusual and personal things often proves to be the most interesting, generating the most compliments and engaging your eye for the longest time.

What style of fireplace goes with what style of room? Should you match it to the architecture or your home furnishings? Do you want a fireplace with a big mantelpiece or a small one? Do you need a mantelpiece at all? Perhaps a simple cut-out surround would suffice – maybe a square or framed circle. You might think that it depends on whether you want to have 'real' flames, but now – with many types of 'designer' fires available, there are almost no rules. The deciding factor might be heat. If you want your fire to heat the room, there are specific products to suit your needs. But there are also requirements to consider concerning flues, chimneys, size of opening, safety and so forth. On the other hand, if it's just the decorative elements that you're after, a flickering flame to look at and a shelf on which to display your trophies – then there are no limits. This might make it easier to decide, or harder. Visit suppliers' showrooms and see what's on offer – and be prepared for a surprise: flames flickering from a row of white pebbles, ceramic pinecones or a jumble of letters of the alphabet; fireplaces that look more like framed artworks or something from a Swiss ski lodge. You can even have a smokeless fire in a glass cylinder in the centre of a coffee table.

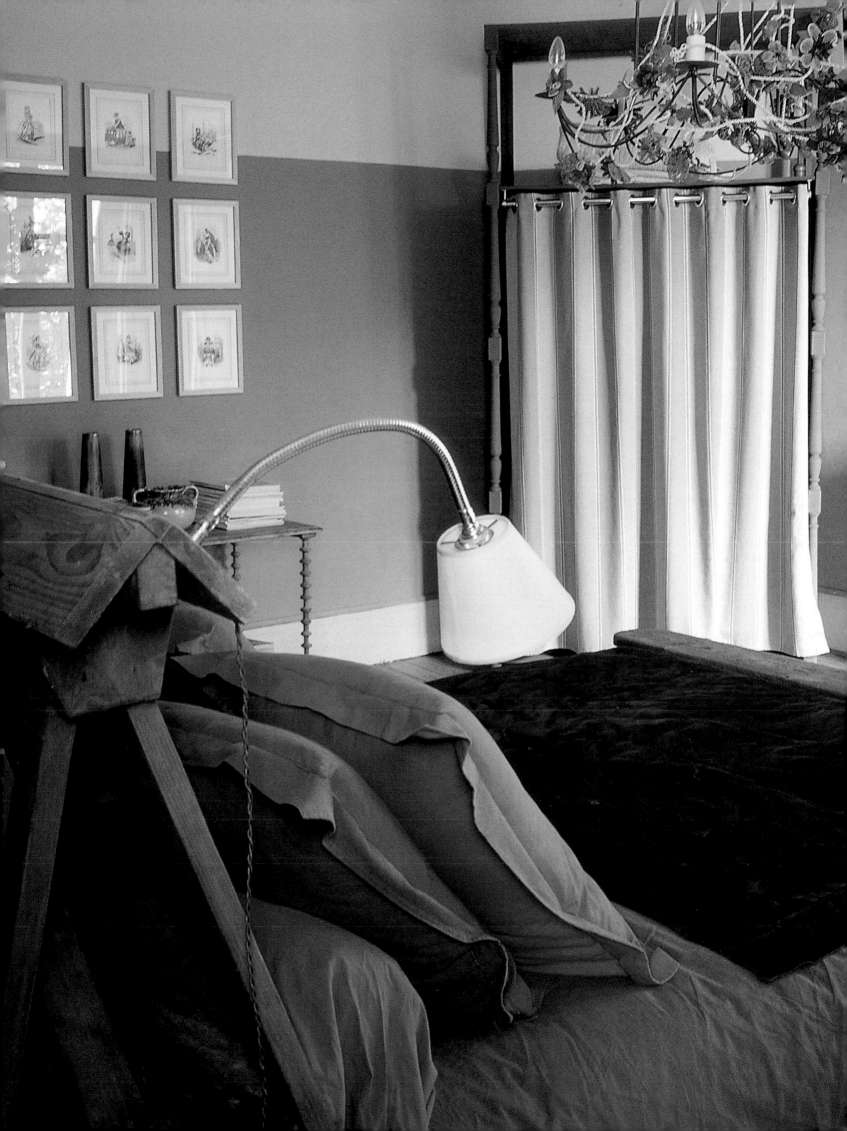

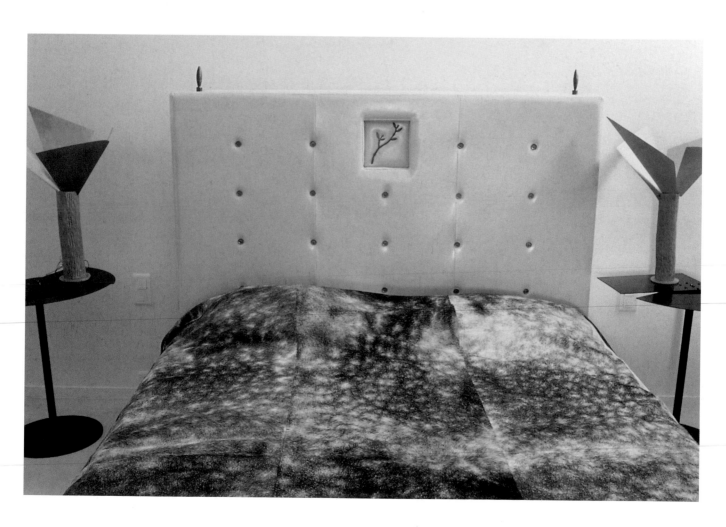

So now you know. No home is ordinary or dull, and nor does it need to be. It's just a matter of opening your eyes and seeing the possibilities. Whether it's a new window, a glass door, an old cupboard or a brightly coloured rug, ideas are everywhere and every homeowner needs as many as they can get. Inspiration can come from visiting a store, a hotel or a country house. But often it's from something in a book, a magazine, or on TV. Sometimes it can be found by simply visiting a neighbour. **Stafford Cliff, London**

The homes on these pages are the loving creations of many people around the world, and I would like to thank all those who, over the last twenty years, have opened their doors and welcomed me into their home so that I could see their treasures. I would also like to express my warmest appreciation to all the architects, designers, decorators, stylists, journalists and assistants who were essential on the photographic shoots. With many special thanks to Stafford Cliff, who has produced a brilliant design from my modest photographs. And also to Jane O'Shea for her enthusiasm and kindness. And, of course, thanks to my wife, Inès, and my two sons, Diego and Kim, for their help and endless patience every day. Christian Sarramon, Paris

Page 16 top and bottom row, centre: Sunfold Systems make high-quality, high-security and highly insulating, sound-deadening aluminium panelled front doors. Design details are highlighted through the use of triple-glazed glass and stainless steel inlays. Their flush surfaces and clear aesthetic lines represent straightforward elegance in its purest form.
Tel: +44 (0) 1953 423423; www.sunfold.com.

Page 17 (except for bottom right): Urban Front are specialist designers and manufacturers of unique, elegant and contemporary doors, made from hardwood and stainless steel. Each door has a reinforced steel core.
Tel: +44 (0) 1494 778787; www.urbanfront.co.uk.

Page 154 fireplaces: top left, from Planika. A series of products that create real fire without any smoke. Incorporates an automatic, electronically controlled ethanol fuel feeding system.
Tel: +48 52 364 11 63; www.planikafires.com.
Top right, from Smart Fire Ltd. The EcoSmart fire is an Australian innovation – an environmentally friendly open fireplace. Flueless, it does not require any installation or utility connection for fuel supply. Fuelled by methylated spirits, it burns cleanly and is virtually maintenance free.
Tel: +44 (0) 20 7173 5014; www.ecosmartfire.com.

Editorial Director Jane O'Shea
Designer Stafford Cliff
Photographer Christian Sarramon
Design Assistant Katherine Case
Editor Laura Herring
Production Vincent Smith, Marina Asenjo

This paperback edition first published in 2009 by
Quadrille Publishing Limited
Alhambra House
27–31 Charing Cross Road
London
WC2H 0LS
www.quadrille.co.uk

Design and layout © 2008
Quadrille Publishing Limited
Photography © 2008 Christian Sarramon
Text © 2008 Stafford Cliff

Cataloguing in Publication Data:
a catalogue record for this book is available from the British Library.

ISBN: 978 184400 746 2

Printed in China